O9-ABI-613

12/15

Vehicles On The Move

Bicycles
Pedal Power

Lynn Peppas

Crabtree Publishing Company

www.crabtreebooks.com

Allen County Public Library

Created by Bobbie Kalman

Author
Lynn Peppas

Editorial director
Kathy Middleton

Project editor
Paul Challen

Editors
Adrianna Morganelli
Crystal Sikkens

Proofreaders
Rachel Stuckey
Janine Belzak

Photo research
Tibor Choleva
Melissa McClellan

Design
Tibor Choleva

Print coordinator
Katherine Berti

Production coordinator
Margaret Amy Salter

Prepress technicians
Margaret Amy Salter
Ken Wright

Consultant
Chad Grochowina, Freewheel Cycle, Dundas Ontario

Illustrations
All illustrations by Leif Peng

Photographs
Bigstock.com: © Vicki France (page 28 top inset); © Robert Beckett (pages 28–29)
© T. Choleva (page 18, page 21)
Dreamstime.com: © Maxim Petrichuk (page 5 bottom); © Brett Pelletier
(page 8); © Maxim Petrichuk (page 9); © Bryan Culbertson (page 11 top);
© Mihalkrol (page 11 bottom); © Khabar (page 20); © Neil Harrison (page
21); © Wolfgang Kaiser (page 25 top); © Jjspring (page 30);
istockphoto: © twilightproductions (page 4); © Mlenny Photography (page 13
top); © hbpstudio (page 16); © ImageegamI (page 27 bottom)
© Melissa McCllellan (page 10)
Photolibrary: Warren Morgan/Flirt Collection: cover
Public Domain: © Secondarywaltz (page 13 bottom); Eric Staller/Conference
bike; © Arriva436 (page 28); © JzG (page 22); © Jim Henderson (page 31
bottom)
Shutterstock.com: © Ljupco Smokovski (title page); © Monkey Business Images
(table of contents page); © BlueOrange Studio (page 5 top); © steamroller_blues
(pages 6–7); © K. Thorsen (page 10); © Rob Wilson (pages 12–13); © Herbert
Kratky (page 12 top); © Willem van de Kerkhof (page 14); © David Hughes
(page 15 top); © zimmytws (page 15 bottom); © Yuriy Davats (page 17
background); © Brocreative (page 19); © Richard Thornton (page 23, pages
24–25); © John Kropewnicki (page 24 inset); © SVLuma (page 26 top); © Zoran
Karapancev (page 26 bottom); © mundoview (page 27 top); © Aija Lehtonen
(page 28 bottom); © Diego Cervo (page 29 top inset); © Olga Besnard (page
31 top)

Library and Archives Canada Cataloguing in Publication

Peppas, Lynn
    Bicycles : pedal power / Lynn Peppas.

(Vehicles on the move)
Includes index.
Issued also in electronic format.
ISBN 978-0-7787-2725-5 (bound).--ISBN 978-0-7787-2732-3 (pbk.)

    1. Bicycles--Juvenile literature. I. Title. II. Series: Vehicles
on the move

TL412.P46 2011   j629.227'2   C2011-900134-9

Library of Congress Cataloging-in-Publication Data

Peppas, Lynn.
    Bicycles : pedal power / Lynn Peppas.
        p. cm. -- (Vehicles on the move)
    Includes index.
    ISBN 978-0-7787-2725-5 (reinforced lib. bdg. : alk. paper) -- ISBN 978-0-
7787-2732-3 (pbk. : alk. paper) -- ISBN 978-1-4271-9694-1 (electronic (PDF))
    1. Bicycles--Juvenile literature. 2. Pedal-powered mechanisms--Juvenile
literature. I. Title.
TL412.P465 2011
629.227'2--dc22
                                              2010052343

Crabtree Publishing Company

Printed in the U.S.A./022011/CJ20101228

www.crabtreebooks.com   1-800-387-7650

Copyright © **2011 CRABTREE PUBLISHING COMPANY**. All rights reserved. No part of this publication may be reproduced, stored in a
retrieval system or be transmitted in any form or by any means, electronic, mechanical, photocopying, recording, or otherwise, without the prior
written permission of Crabtree Publishing Company. In Canada: We acknowledge the financial support of the Government of Canada through the
Canada Book Fund for our publishing activities.

Published in Canada
Crabtree Publishing
616 Welland Ave.
St. Catharines, ON
L2M 5V6

Published in the United States
Crabtree Publishing
PMB 59051
350 Fifth Avenue, 59th Floor
New York, New York 10118

Published in the United Kingdom
Crabtree Publishing
Maritime House
Basin Road North, Hove
BN41 1WR

Published in Australia
Crabtree Publishing
386 Mt. Alexander Rd.
Ascot Vale (Melbourne)
VIC 3032

Contents

Bicycles

Vehicles are machines that carry people from one place to another. Bicycles are vehicles that are good, clean, and fun. Bicycles are good exercise. They are clean for the environment. They are quiet and easy to ride in cities where there is a lot of **traffic**. And bicycle riding is fun!

Family bike rides are a great way to burn off some energy and have fun together.

"Bi" means two

Bicycles have two wheels that follow in a single line. There are different kinds of bicycles for riding on different kinds of surfaces. Bicycles come in different sizes for riders of all ages. A person who rides a bicycle is called a cyclist. Sometimes bicycles are called bikes.

training wheels

Training wheels can be attached to bicycles for small children.

Mountain bikes are built for off-road cycling. Their frames are strong but very lightweight.

Pedal power!

Bicycles are powered to move by people pushing pedals. Cyclists push the pedals forward. Pedals turn arms called cranks. The cranks move the chain. The chain moves the back wheel and the bicycle moves forward.

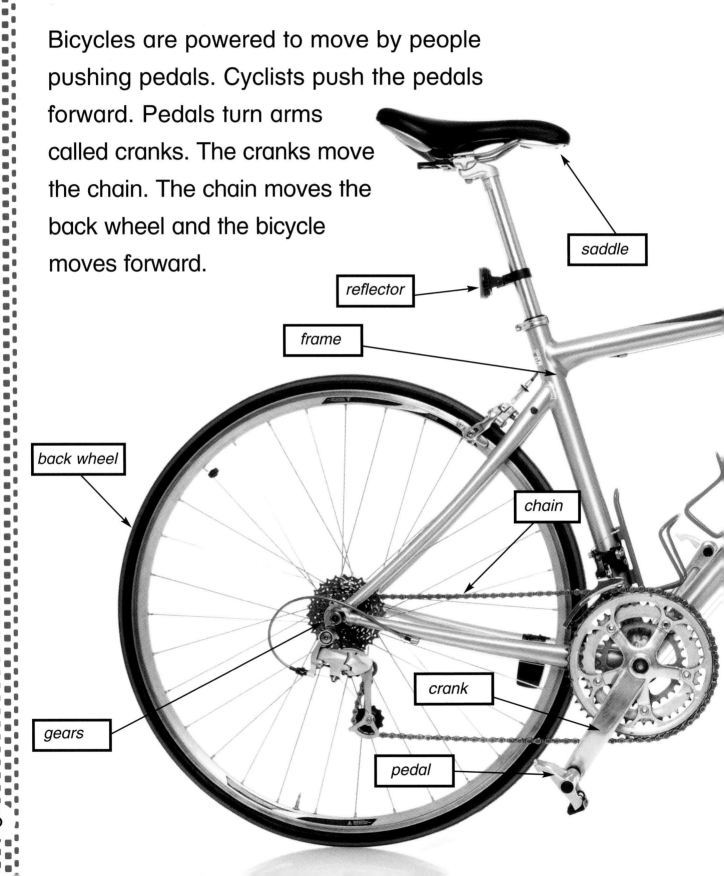

saddle

reflector

frame

back wheel

chain

gears

crank

pedal

Bicycles have sturdy frames made of hollow steel tubes. They have brakes that allow the cyclist to stop. On some bikes, the cyclist pedals backward to stop. Sometimes the brakes are located on the handlebars. The rider squeezes the lever to stop.

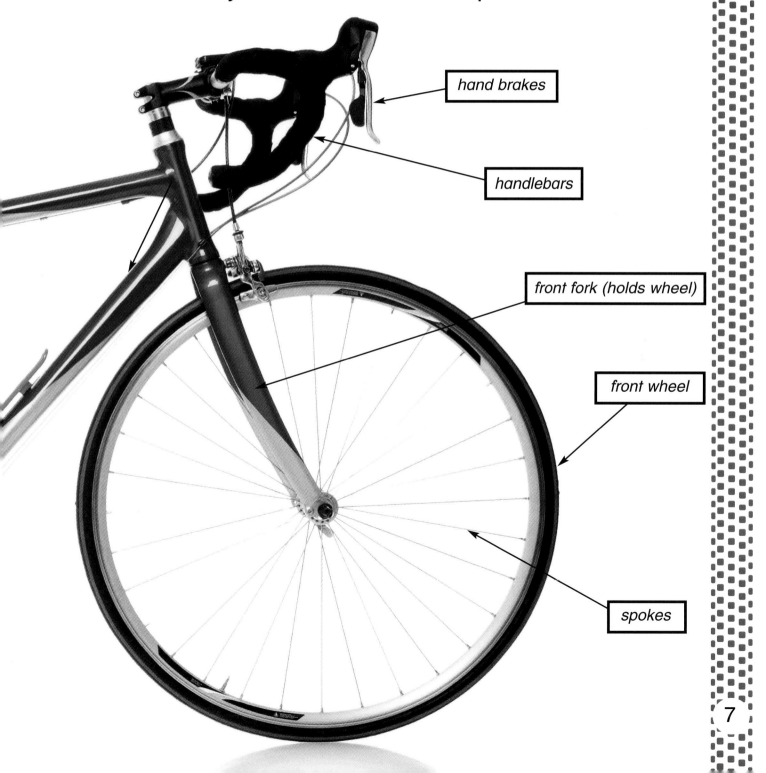

hand brakes

handlebars

front fork (holds wheel)

front wheel

spokes

Mountain bikes

Mountain bikes are very sturdy. They are sometimes called ATBs. This stands for all-terrain bicycle. ATBs are made to travel over all kinds of dirt surfaces or **terrain**. They have wide, knobby tires and gears. A cyclist changes gears to make pedaling easier when going up hills.

Mountain bike trails can be dangerous for new riders. It takes a lot of practice and experience to be able to ride the trails safely.

Bumps or hills

Cross-country
bicycling is a sport.
Cyclists race their bicycles
through nature trails. It is not
as easy as riding on smooth
roads. Cyclists ride through
bumpy or hilly areas.

Stunt bicycles

Ready for some extreme cycling? Then a **stunt bicycle** is the vehicle for you! Stunt bicycles are often called BMX bikes. BMX stands for bicycle motocross. It is a sport where cyclists race on dirt tracks over different kinds of terrain and obstacles.

BMX races are divided from beginners to expert, based on a rider's age and experience.

Tricky stuff!

Freestyle BMX is doing stunts on a stunt bicycle. Stunts are special tricks. Some BMX bikes have special equipment for stunts, such as pegs. Pegs are used for tricks called grinds. In a grind, the bicycle moves on the peg instead of the wheel.

a peg

Stunt bicycles are used for tricks, such as grinds on human-made obstacles.

BMX cyclists use ramps to do stunts in the air.

Racing bicycles

Racing bicycles are made to travel fast. They are lightweight and have thin tires. Racing bicycles are made to travel on road or track surfaces. They are not as comfortable as other bicycles, but they are faster.

Some racing bicycles have a solid disk wheel. It helps them go faster.

In a road race, cyclists start in a large group. The group slowly breaks apart as faster racers speed ahead.

Beating the wind

You can tell a racing bicycle by its curly handlebars. Handlebars curl down and toward the bicycle. A cyclist leans into the wind to grip the handlebars. Doing this makes them travel faster. When cyclists sit upright, the wind pushes against them. This slows them down.

Indoor bicycle races are held on a track inside a stadium called a velodrome.

Tandem Bicycles

A **tandem bicycle** seats more than one cyclist. Tandem means that two people sit one behind the other. Most tandem bicycles seat only two. Some can seat three, four, or even more cyclists.

child seat

child seat

adult seat

This tandem bicycle is designed for one adult and two children. These bikes are a great way for parents and kids to have fun together!

Let's double up!

The cyclist in the very front of a tandem bicycle steers with the handlebars. He or she also pedals to move the bicycle forward. Riders behind the front cyclist use the handlebars to balance themselves. They push pedals to help move forward, too.

Some tandem bicycles can seat more than two riders.

A tandem bicycle can be an inexpensive recreational vehicle. Riding with another person can be a lot of fun.

Party bicycles

Some bicycles let more than one cyclist sit side by side instead of in a line. This kind of bicycle is called a sociable. Sociable means people talk and keep each other company.

Riding a four-wheeled bike is a fun and safe way to go sightseeing.

Street conference

A party bicycle can seat up to seven people. Everyone faces each other around a circle. It has four wheels altogether. There are two in the front, and a double wheel in the back. Everyone has pedals to help move the bike forward. The cyclist at the back of the bike steers with a steering wheel.

This party bike is called a ConferenceBike. Up to seven people can ride together and have fun talking to each other.

Trailer bikes

A **trailer bike** is perfect for very young cyclists. It is pulled by another bicycle in front. It has a tow bar that hooks up to the bicycle that will pull it. A trailer bike carries one young rider.

A trailer bike has one back wheel, a seat, and pedals to help move it forward. It also has handlebars for the rider to hold on to.

trailer bike

bicycle

attachment hitch

The child's handlebars on a trailer bike are for balance. They do not help steer the bicycle.

Along for the ride

A bicycle trailer is a wheeled frame with a hitch. It can be used for transporting cargo by bicycle. Some trailers can carry as much as 1000 pounds (454 kg) of cargo. Family bike trailers are built to allow adults to safely include children on bike trips.

safety flag

bike trailer

bike

attachment hitch

Bicycle trailers have light reflectors and a safety flag to make it easier for cars and other cyclists to see them.

Unicycles

A **unicycle** is a one-wheeled vehicle. "Uni" means one. It has pedals and a seat above the wheel, just like a bicycle. But it does not have handlebars. Cyclists must use their balance to ride a unicycle.

These tall unicycles are called giraffe unicycles. They are the most common unicycles used in parades and shows.

Solo rider

Unicycles come in different styles such as stunt unicycles and mountain unicycles. Unicycles have no gears. The riders cannot change gears to make riding uphill easier.

On a monocycle, the cyclist sits inside a single wheel instead of on top.

Mountain unicycling is a fast-growing sport.

Recumbent bicycles

Cyclists on a **recumbent bicycle** look like they are lying down while riding. That's because they are! Recumbent means lying down. The seat is tilted back and low to the ground. Most recumbent bicycle pedals sit on top of the front wheel.

Recumbent bikes can go faster than everyday bikes.

Built for speed

Recumbent bicycles are the fastest type of bicycle. This is because they are **aerodynamic**. Aerodynamic means the cyclist cuts into the wind instead of pushing against it.

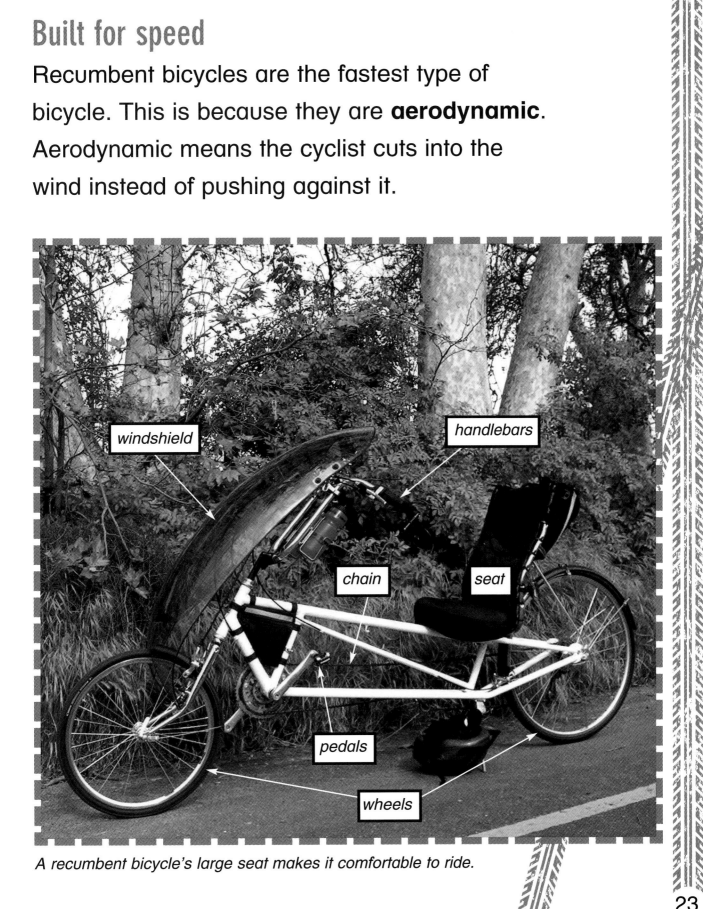

A recumbent bicycle's large seat makes it comfortable to ride.

Handcycles

Handcycles are powered by arms instead of legs. Most handcycles are three-wheeled bicycles. Handcycles have handholds that work like pedals. A cyclist pushes the handholds around to power the bike. Handholds help to steer and stop the bicycles, too.

bicycle

Handy riders

There are different types of handcycles. Some are sturdier and can be used for mountain cycling. Lightweight handcycles can be used for long road trips or racing. Riding a handcycle is a good way to increase upper body strength.

Handcycles are especially useful for people who cannot use their legs to ride a bicycle.

handcycle

Bicycles at work

People ride bicycles at work, too. Police officers ride bicycles where there might be a lot of traffic or crowds of people. A rickshaw is a bicycle with three wheels used to drive people around in big cities.

A rickshaw is sometimes called a bikecab.

Police officers in cities use specially built police bicycles. Police bicycles are mountain bikes that are adjusted to fit the needs of police departments.

Delivering the goods

A bicycle messenger is sometimes called a bicycle courier. They ride bicycles to deliver lightweight letters and packages in large cities. Bike messengers can get through traffic jams easily. It is easy for them to park their bicycles.

In some countries, people use bicycles instead of cars or trucks.

Bike couriers deliver letters and small parcels in crowded city streets. They can deliver the goods in a short amount of time and in any weather.

Bikes and big cities

Many cyclists use bicycles to get around in big cities. Some roads have bicycle lanes where only cyclists are allowed. Public transportation buses sometimes have special racks for bikes. When cyclists get off the bus they can ride their bikes again.

This picture shows a bike rack on a bus.

Some cities are better for biking than others. Biking is the favorite way to get around Amsterdam, in the Netherlands.

Sharing the ride

Some large cities have bike-sharing stations. Cyclists use these bikes to ride to different places in the city. They leave them at a different bike-sharing station for another cyclist to use. Cyclists pay a small fee to use the bikes.

The bike-sharing system in Paris, France, is called Vélib'. It has 10,000 bikes to share at 750 stations.

Electric bicycles

Electric bicycles, or E-bikes, have an electric motor that moves them forward when cyclists take a break from pedaling. The motor gets power from **rechargeable** batteries. Batteries are fueled by plugging them into outlets. They can also be fueled at charging stations.

Electric bicycles are a very common form of transportation in Asia. People use them to shop for groceries, too.

Combining the power

A pedelec is a bicycle that also has an electric motor. The electric motor on the pedelec is used to help cyclists pedal. It does not replace pedaling. Cyclists move the bike forward by pedaling. The electric motor also moves the bike forward. This is helpful when riding long distances or up hills.

Electric bikes are a good way to get around busy cities and they do not create any pollution.

Electric bikes come in different shapes and designs. They all have electric motors that move them forward. E-bikes can travel at speeds of about 20 mph (32 km/h).

Words to know and Index

electric bicycle
pages 30–31

recumbent bicycle
pages 22–23

stunt bicycle
pages 10–11

tandem bicycle
pages 14–15

Other index words

trailer bicycle
page 18

unicycle
pages 20–21